365 Quotes and Meditations

Spiritual, Life and Death

VICTOR DE LA FUENTE

365 Quotes and Meditations

SPIRITUAL, LIFE AND DEATH

Víctor de la Fuente

365 Quotes and Meditations – Spiritual, Life and Death / Víctor de la Fuente. – 1st Edition

ISBN 978-1728993539

Index

PROLOGUE

THE QUOTES. THE INSPIRATION.

ABOUT THE AUTHOR

OTHER BOOKS BY THE AUTHOR

Prologue

Since my early adulthood, I collected phrases and concepts that awakened "something" in me really caught my attention. Sometimes it was simple curiosity. Others created a seed that in time would mold a way of thinking, values or an ideology. This collection is a selection of quotes, concepts, aphorisms, reflections and arguments that marked me in one way or another.

In the collection, I mostly include modern authors. That way I avoid overused classic phrases from writers, thinkers and personalities. This isn't a mass-produced book as a result of copying/pasting the most famous quotes. Paradoxically, this is a very personal book, even though not all words are mine and I speak through others. The book contains modern philosophy based on modern philosophers, essays in a wide range of themes, and even fiction and pop culture, too. In some cases, the quote has no author. In those cases, it's mostly because there's no assignable author and because the quotes are my own reaping both in their whole originality and their adaptation.

Among the different volumes of the collection, no quote is repeated so, even when there are common and comparable lessons among topics, there's no repeated quote and therefore, original and unique material in each volume.

There are many ways to enjoy the following pages. One of the options is to read a quote each day, take it in and reflect on that concept. Another option would be to work each phrase particularly, taking advantage of the space between one another for annotations and personal reflections. And finally, all at once. Depending on the objective that each person has, they will take more or less advantage one way or another.

In any case, in order to internalize the concepts, repetition is key. Precisely with that goal in mind, concepts are referenced in different ways all along the book. Besides, an approach to a concept will awaken interest in some people in a way and attract others in another. At the same time, it shouldn't be a surprise when a concept is quoted different times proclaiming different philosophies. More with the intent to force the reflection rather than pleasing every public, this way we manage to test our beliefs while generating discussion, and probably confirm that there isn't a sole correct perception about determined topics.

It's hard to separate the "pseudo-" from revolutionary things. Even more to separate a superficial, instant gratification from a deeper thought. Without further ado, I invite the reader to get into the reflections that I hope will provoke them as much as they provoked me.

The quotes. The inspiration.

Appreciating the present moment is as simple as noticing the sensations around you.

What an oxymoron - rarity in everything.

Sam Lustgarten

Book: Frugaling

Alert to world's beauty.

William Braxton Irving

Book: A guide to the good life

The probability of your existence.

I've been so focus on where I'm going that I didn't notice where I was.

Aubrey

Movie: The first time

What we see is temporary but what we don't see is Eternal.

Nature is not balanced.

Slavoj Zizek

Book: Demanding the impossible

Being 'in the world but not of it' is not an ideal state of existence.

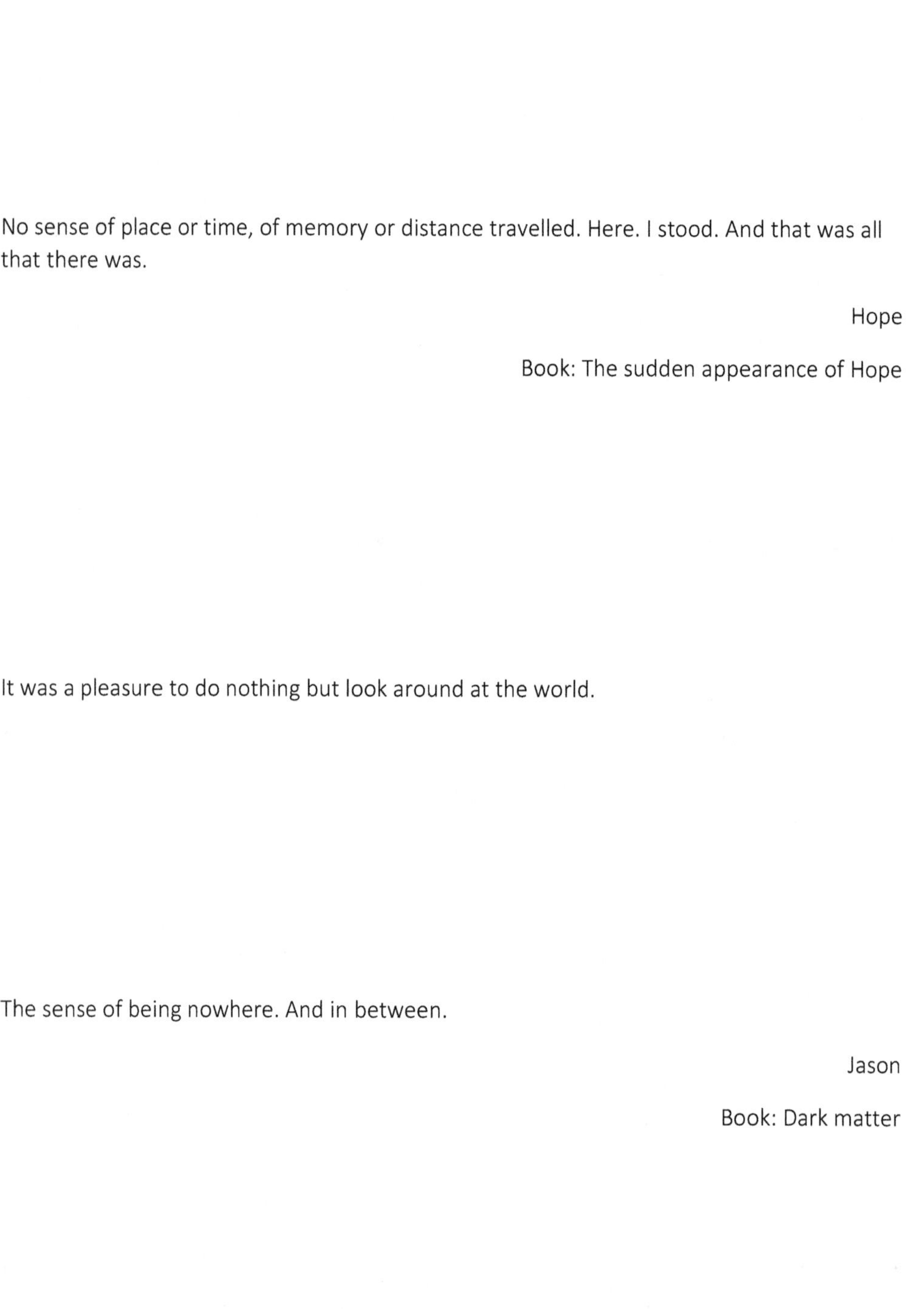

No sense of place or time, of memory or distance travelled. Here. I stood. And that was all that there was.

Hope

Book: The sudden appearance of Hope

It was a pleasure to do nothing but look around at the world.

The sense of being nowhere. And in between.

Jason

Book: Dark matter

The believer needs no third-party verifiable evidence at all: inner conviction suffices.

Julian Baggini

Book: The edge of reason

Don't you see that we can't have our eyes closed and be able to see out there?

David Eagleman

Book: Incognito

Do all gods feel so lonely?

Daenerys Targaryen

Book: Tormenta de espadas

A nomad in my own heart.

They fear being loved because it does make them more vulnerable and aware of their mortality.

Ataraxia, a state of perfect mental tranquility.

Observe the sensations of the moment. Don't think about those sensations, just experience them.

Leave your mind; enter the moment.

The non-religious do not find meaning, purpose and value by taking a leap into the unknown. We find it in the beauty and joy of life.

Good habits are something that must be learned, but can't be taught.

Gretchen Rubin

Book: Better than before

The invisible architecture of daily life.

Gretchen Rubin

Book: Better than before

It's just one story.

Rust Cohle

TV-Series: True Detective

'I can die happy'. But this invites the serious reply, 'Why not?'

Julian Baggini

Book: What's it all about?

Water only travels in one direction.

Christopher McDougall

Book: Natural born heroes

Atheism is not a faith position because all that can't be 100% proven is not equally unproven.

Julian Baggini

The echoing sounds of silence.

Science has proven to be the most reliable guide to truth.

The lottery of existence. The genetic lottery.

Leave 10% of your luggage space for what the journey has to offer.

How to love the wind. Wind extinguishes a candle and energizes fire.

Nassim Nicholas Taleb

Book: Antifragile

Why the sun was just then setting over the river.

Kerry Howley

Book: Thrown

Silence is an answer too.

Strangers in a strange land.

Hope

Book: The sudden appearance of Hope

A mind that will not stop, thoughts that will not cease.

Kepler

Book: Touch

The holistic nature of understanding: any single thing we believe is connected, web-like, to any number of other beliefs.

Julian Baggini

Book: The pig that wants to be eaten

To be completely present in the moment.

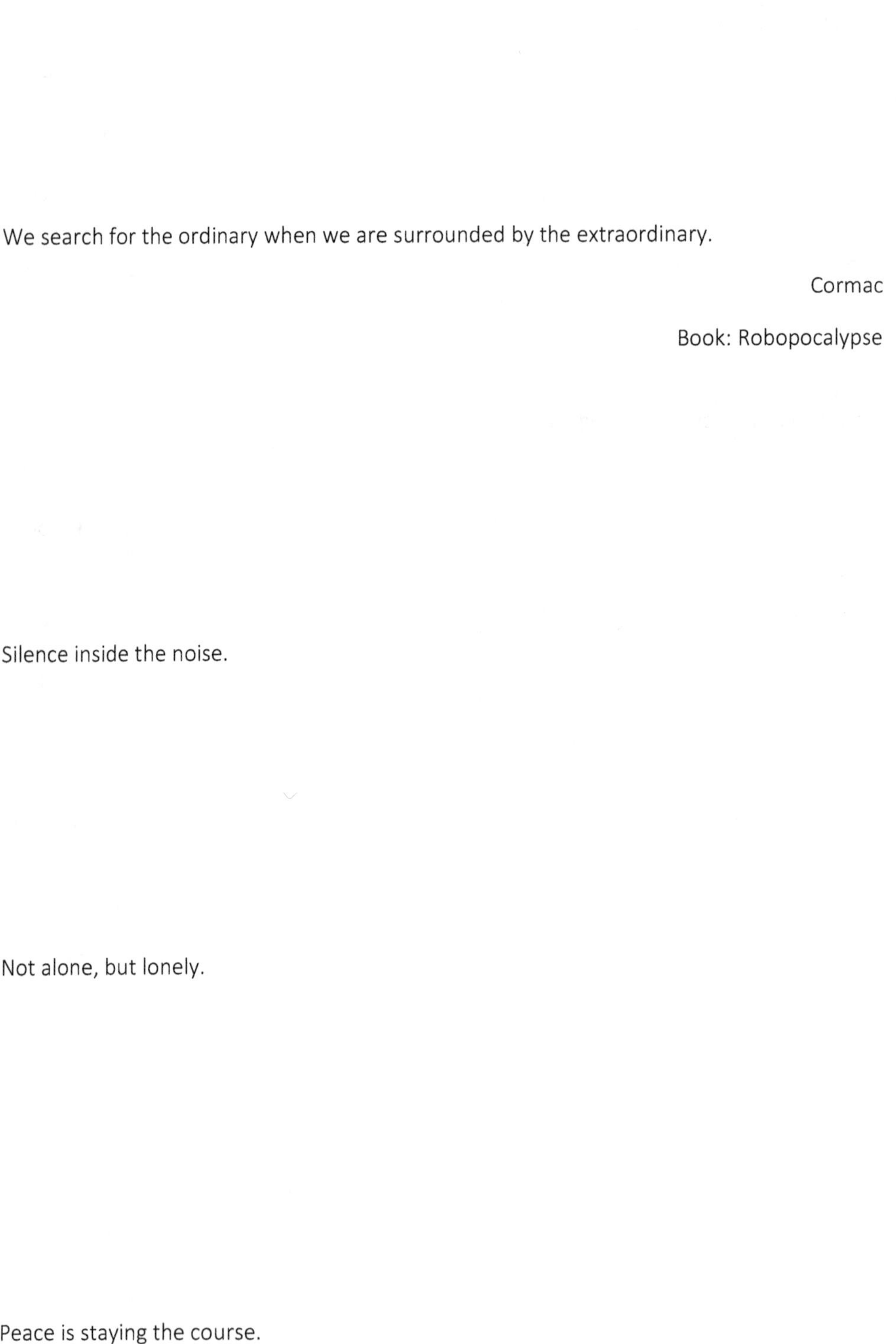

We search for the ordinary when we are surrounded by the extraordinary.

Cormac

Book: Robopocalypse

Silence inside the noise.

Not alone, but lonely.

Peace is staying the course.

Ryan Holiday

Book: The daily stoic

The question. So if that was it, would you be satisfied with how you'd pursued your life? Yes.

Rich Roll

Book: Finding Ultra

Marks of the good life.

Ryan Holiday

Book: The daily stoic

Be good and noble and impressive now —while it still matters.

Ryan Holiday

Book: The daily stoic

Lonely, but not alone.

A meeting of the minds rather than a touching of bodies.

Michael Finkel

Book: Stranger in the woods

Love without sacrifice is theft.

Nassim Nicholas Taleb

Book: Skin the game

The universe answered him with silence.

Henry Marco

Book: The Return Man

First to 'Be'; then to 'Become'; and ultimately to no longer 'Be'.

We're as ephemeral as raindrops. We all fall, and we all land somewhere.

Jason Lawton

Book: Spin

We are alive, and then we are not. We move on. Who knows to where? Eventually, someone else will be living in our apartments, in our city, in our world, and we'll be off and away. We all have different paths, 2-B. But we share the same future, don't we? Which is why we are here for each other.

Windy

TV-Series: Life on Mars US

Love is for the living.

Don't be sorry. Why should you apologize? You should be thankful. You have an abundance of feeling.

Dr. Gaius Baltar

TV-Series: Battlestar Galactica

Time waits for no one.

Makoto Konno

Movie: The girl who leapt through time

Love should never be a secret.

Dr. Otto Octavius

Movie: Spiderman 2

Even the most seemingly random events have logic behind them.

Max

Movie: Good Time Max

Life has a melody, Gaius. A rhythm of notes which become your existence once played in harmony with God's plan.

Number Six

TV-Series: Battlestar Galactica

It's the sense of touch. In any real city, you walk, you know? You brush past people, people bump into you. In L.A., nobody touches you. We're always behind this metal and glass. I think we miss that touch so much, that we crash into each other, just so we can feel something.

Daniel

Movie: Crash

The music is the wind.

So massive was the commitment to their beliefs that no other truth was tolerable.

Robert Cialdini

Book: Influence The Psychology of Persuasion

I love the word "mamihlapinatapai." That moment or feeling when two people both want to initiate something but neither wants to be the one to start it.

Woman

Movie: Life in a Day.

Don't think you're not crying because there's no teardrops in your eyes.

The universe is indifferent.

Donald Draper

TV-Series: Mad Men

That intensely alive state that is free of time, free of problems, free of thinking, free of the burden of the personality.

Eckhart Tolle

Book: The Power of Now

Chaos is harder to embrace. It's scary to think there's no one out there looking out for us.

Friend's Max

Movie: Good Time Max

I looked again at the stars. They had no opinion on the matter.

Scott Jurek

Book: Eat and run

The light of the sun is not selective.

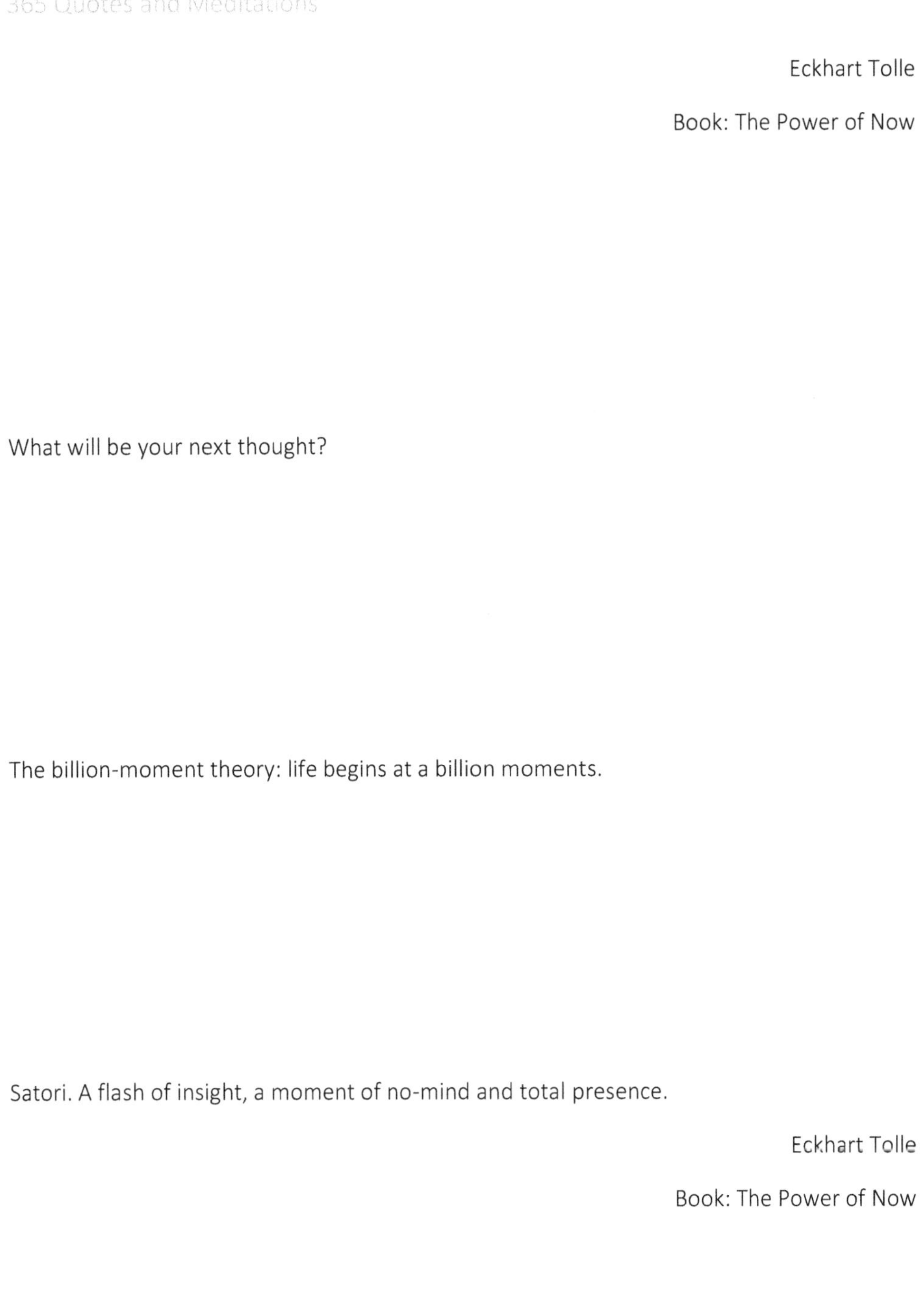

Eckhart Tolle

Book: The Power of Now

What will be your next thought?

The billion-moment theory: life begins at a billion moments.

Satori. A flash of insight, a moment of no-mind and total presence.

Eckhart Tolle

Book: The Power of Now

But again, since different religions make different moral demands of people, if many religions are true, God must be a relativist, for he requires different things for Jews, Hindus, Sikhs, Muslims, Christians and members of any other religion.

Julian Baggini

Book: The big questions: ethics

Coincidence is by definition meaningless. And yet coincidence is a part of life rocking existence then vanishing absurdly as it arrived.

Roobert McKee

Book: Story: Substance, Structure, Style, and the Principles of Screenwriting

Your fellow traveler in life.

Brian R. Little

Book: Me, myself and us

Our life is the manifestation of our minds.

Dan Harris

Book: 10% Happier

Learn how to be happy "before anything happens".

Dan Harris

Book: 10% Happier

Life's in-between moments.

Dan Harris

Book: 10% Happier

Nobody knows what they are doing. They just go along.

Indifference is a power, selectively applied, and living in such a way is, with a conscious adoption of certain attitudes, a freer, more expansive, more adventurous mode of living.

Life can only be a meaningless accident of nature.

Julian Baggini

Book: What's it all about?

The genetic fallacy: the mistake is to think that understanding the origins of life automatically tells us its end goal or present purpose.

Julian Baggini

Book: What's it all about?

When coincidence rules story, it creates a new and rather significant meaning: Life is absurd.

Robert McKee

Book: Story: Substance, Structure, Style, and the Principles of Screenwriting

Unexpected forms of magic.

Deus ex Machina is an insult because it is a lie.

Robert McKee

Book: Story: Substance, Structure, Style, and the Principles of Screenwriting

Beyond happiness, becoming whole.

Todd Kashdan

Book: The upside of your dark side

Does God command what is good because it is good, or are things only good because God commands them?

Julian Baggini

Book: The big questions: ethics

Divine command theory: those actions are made right or wrong only by God's decree, they are not right or wrong in themselves.

Julian Baggini

Book: The big questions: ethics

As I discovered more about myself, I realized that I interpreted my emotions rather than actually experiencing them.

Think about what you need, not what you want.

Even if God is by definition good, we can still ask if it is through being good that God is by definition good, or whether it is by being a property of God that good is defined as it is.

Julian Baggini

Book: The big questions: ethics

365 Quotes and Meditations

When was the last time you took a walk around the lake?

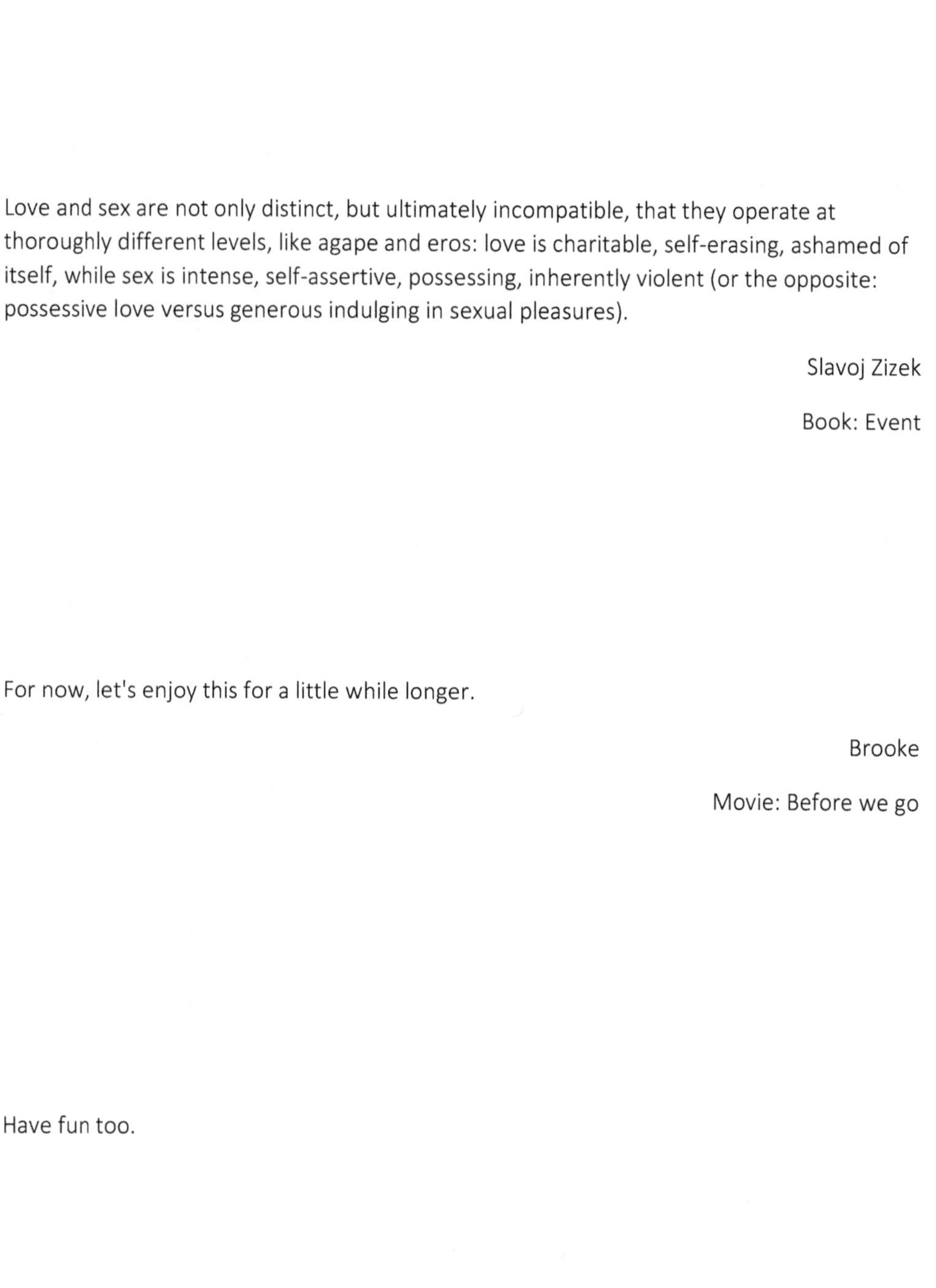

Love and sex are not only distinct, but ultimately incompatible, that they operate at thoroughly different levels, like agape and eros: love is charitable, self-erasing, ashamed of itself, while sex is intense, self-assertive, possessing, inherently violent (or the opposite: possessive love versus generous indulging in sexual pleasures).

Slavoj Zizek

Book: Event

For now, let's enjoy this for a little while longer.

Brooke

Movie: Before we go

Have fun too.

I do great things to live and enjoy the little ones.

You only live once, but if you work it right, once is enough.

Joe Louis in Dean Karnazes

Book: Ultramarathon man

Do I feel alive?

Laura Moon

TV-Series: American gods

No single window can reveal the entire panorama.

Edward Russo

Book: Winning decisions

The fiasco of God is still the fiasco of God.

Slavoj Zizek

Book: Event

Another world is possible.

Slavoj Zizek

Book: Demanding the impossible

I like the way I'm starting to walk.

Inmate

Doc: At Night I Fly

The paradox about human nature and its defense system is this: Most of us try to control life by protecting ourselves from it. A complementary paradox is that not taking risks might well be the greatest risk of all. Another complementary paradox, if you can surrender to the fact that you -and everybody's else's –vulnerability, recognizing that regardless of the outcome you'll almost certainly survive, you'll then experience yourself as less vulnerable. On the contrary, the more energy you put into protecting yourself from uncomfortable feelings of jeopardy, the more vulnerable you'll end up feeling.

There is no such thing as addiction. There is only things that you enjoy doing more than life.

Doug Stanhope

Stand-up comedy: Before turning the gun on himself

It's just the end of the day.

Grant Mazzy

Movie: Pontypool

Life should be awesome.

The 'Western Buddhist' meditative path is arguably the most efficient way for us to fully participate in capitalist dynamics while retaining the appearance of mental sanity.

Slavoj Zizek

Book: Event

The true horror does not occur when we are abandoned by God, but when God comes too close to us.

Slavoj Zizek

Book: Event

I do not love you because I find your positive features attractive, but, on the contrary, I find your positive features attractive because I love you.

Slavoj Zizek

Book: Event

A true love is enough in itself, it makes sex irrelevant – but precisely because 'fundamentally, it doesn't matter', we can fully enjoy it without any superego pressure.

Slavoj Zizek

Book: Event

The serpent promises Adam and Eve that, by eating the fruit of the tree of knowledge, they will become like God; and after the two do it, God says: 'Behold, Adam has become like one of us' (Genesis 3:22). Hegel's comment is: 'So the serpent did not lie, for God confirms what it said.'

Slavoj Zizek

Book: Event

God exists only insofar as he doesn't know (take note of, register) his own inexistence. The moment God knows, he collapses into the abyss of inexistence, like the familiar cartoon cat which falls only when it notices there is no ground beneath its feet.

Slavoj Zizek

Book: Less than nothing

The one who waked up.

Joseph Campbell

Book: The power of myth

Focus, calm and clarity.

The problem with heaven is that you will be having such a good time there, you won't even think of eternity.

Joseph Campbell

Book: The power of myth

I exist for the world, and the world exists for me.

Bruce Lee

Book: Striking thoughts

An extinction-level event would, in an existential flash, make our down-to-earth struggles irrelevant.

Elon Musk

A person cannot forget someone who is good to them.

Bruce Lee

Book: Striking thoughts

There is a difference between contemplating something bad happening and worrying about it.

William Braxton Irving

Book: A guide to the good life

Who had only begun to love, who had not yet had the chance to test the limits of that love, or of life itself.

Jeff Winston

Book: Replay

Contemplating heaven while living on earth.

Bruce Lee

Book: Striking thoughts

I no longer covet paradise. More important, I no longer fear hell.

Bruce Lee

Book: Striking thoughts

Creating new memories stretches out psychological time, and lengthens our perception of our lives.

Joshua Foer

Book: Moonwalking with Einstein

Embracing the full range of human experiences -the positive and the negative.

Todd Kashdan

Book: Curious?

The "true" fans respected these natural changes.

Todd Kashdan

Book: Curious?

Just live.

I did love like a madman, but have enough sense to not love as a fool.

Bruce Lee

Book: Striking thoughts

Don't add worry to your troubles.

Bruce Lee

Book: Striking thoughts

Worry only creates problems for those around you.

Bruce Lee

Book: Striking thoughts

I am not the subject of an experience; I am that experience.

Bruce Lee

Book: Striking thoughts

Live life like a legend.

We need death to give shape and meaning to life. Without it, we would find life pointless. On this view, if hell is eternal damnation, the eternity of life in Hades would be enough to make it a place of punishment.

Julian Baggini

Book: The pig that wants to be eaten

Am I the only fully qualified expert on how to live my life?

Julian Baggini

Book: The pig that wants to be eaten

The universe is infinite. And so are the possibilities of my life.

Daniel Eakins

Book: The man who folded himself

There is no actor but the action - there is no experiencer but experience.

Bruce Lee

Book: Striking thoughts

A story is about significant events and memorable moments, not about time passing.

Daniel Kahneman

Book: Thinking , Fast and Slow

Faith might lead you to believe in miracles, but reason can never follow suit.

Stephen Law and Julian Baggini

Book: 30-Second philosophies

Greatness in the Moment.

Brian P. Moran

Book: The 12 Week year

We are all responsible for what the future holds in store. Thus it is our duty, not to prophesy evil but, rather, to fight for a better world.

Karl Popper in David Deutsch

Book: The beginning of infinity

The best of all possible worlds.

Michael Shermer

Book: Why people believe weird things

The nonexistence after death will be much like it was before birth, which I didn't find at all dissatisfying.

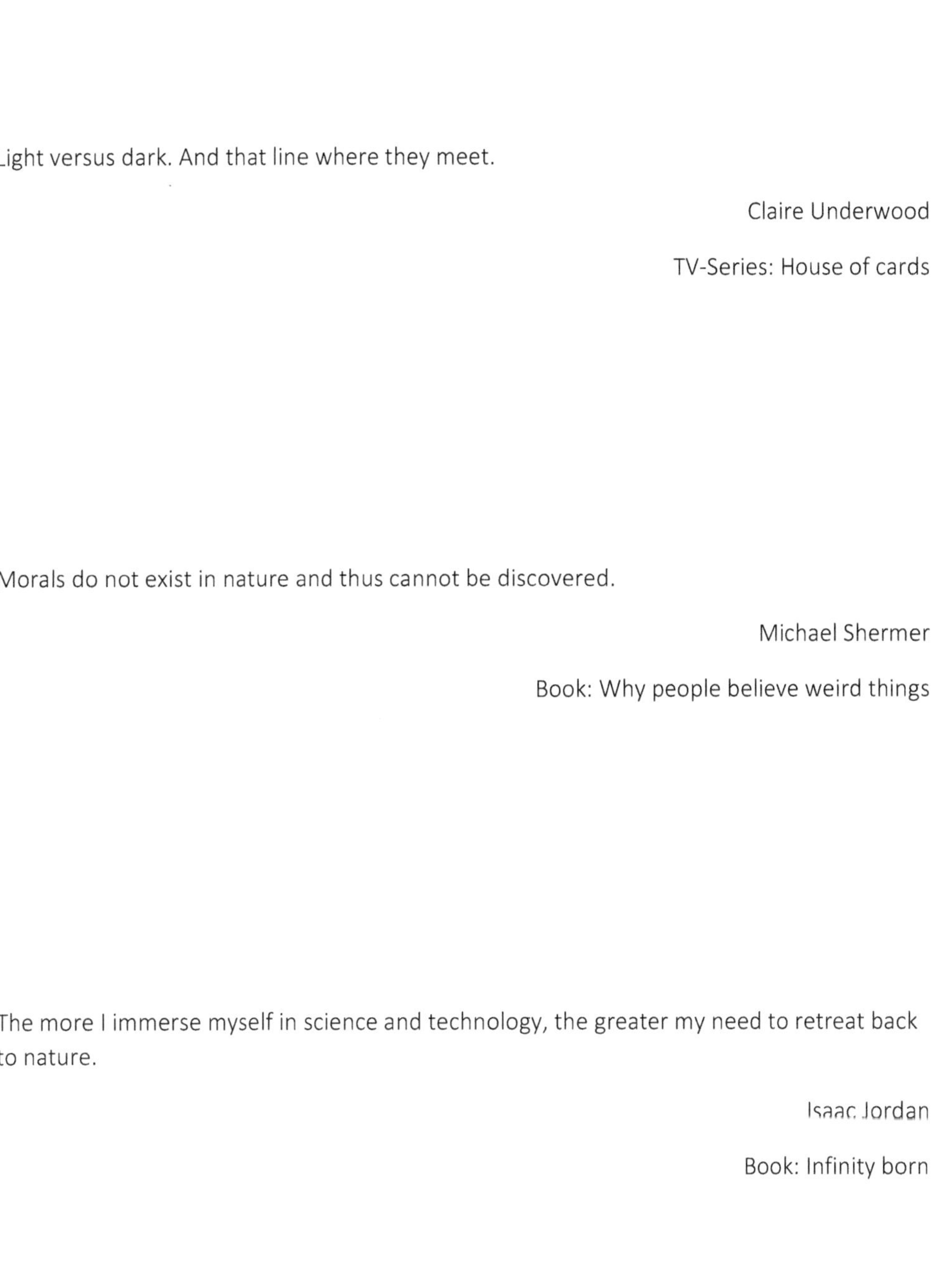

Light versus dark. And that line where they meet.

Claire Underwood

TV-Series: House of cards

Morals do not exist in nature and thus cannot be discovered.

Michael Shermer

Book: Why people believe weird things

The more I immerse myself in science and technology, the greater my need to retreat back to nature.

Isaac Jordan

Book: Infinity born

In the watching lies the wonder.

Bruce Lee

Book: Striking thoughts

The watching is a state of "being" already, not a state of becoming.

Bruce Lee

Book: Striking thoughts

The preference for meaning over pleasure gets stronger as we focus more on the distant future.

Todd Kashdan

Book: The upside of your dark side

Boredom is often an important indicator that you are making poor choices, or entering new situations with a limiting attitude.

Todd Kashdan

Book: The upside of your dark side

Relax, you've made it.

Daniel Coyle

Book: The little book of talent

You know what would be nice?

Sam Lustgarten

Book: Frugaling

The infinite god of nothing.

Charles Seife

Book: Zero

Is it better to be slaves with a role in the universe or to be free people left to create a role for ourselves?

Julian Baggini

Book: What's it all about?

A willingness to let our morals be guided by the facts.

Julian Baggini

Book: A short history of truth

Right here. Right now. Just as we are. Nothing to prove.

As long as you're happy.

Julian Baggini

Book: What's it all about?

Religion does not just promote different truths, it advocates different grounds of truth. The truth of religion is something many believers feel almost viscerally. It connects to their very sense of self, identity and belonging. It is as much, or more, felt than thought.

Julian Baggini

Book: A short history of truth

If, however, the altruist starts to see helping others as itself the most important thing in life, then they are actually undermining the values their altruism itself asserts. How can a person claim both that everyone ought to live a full life free from suffering and that in his own case it is more important to help others than to live such a life? Guilty of inconsistency.

Julian Baggini

Book: What's it all about?

The most ordinary moments are the ones that are the most transcendent.

Helping others cannot therefore be the meaning of life itself. But it is essentially tied to the meaningful life, because it is premised on the notion that life can be a good in itself. If this is true for one it is true for all, and so we have reasons for helping others. Altruism in thus not the source of life's meaning but is something that living a meaningful life requires. We just need to remember that the purpose of helping others is to bring them benefits, not to engage in charity for charity's sake.

Julian Baggini

Book: What's it all about?

You should never seduce a person whose life you cannot improve.

Crew Spence

Book: The ethical pickup artist

The moon came up. It was the only time when my mind could just be quiet.

Superman

Comic: Superman Earth One

Mindfulness and awareness.

Sakyong Mipham Rinpoche

Book: Running with the Mind of Meditation

Giving you just enough sound to hear the silence and just enough light to realize how dark it really is.

Narrator

Documentary: Fear itself

Silence and darkness are just names we give to the moments when our eyes and ears let us down. If I look out into the night and can't see anything, it doesn't mean there's nothing, just nothing I can't make out.

Narrator

Documentary: Fear itself

No definitive end, just a flowing into a space that is bigger, wider, and deeper than where we began.

Jerry Lynch

Book: Running within

I recharge in the quiet.

Stillness in motion.

Jerry Lynch

Book: Running within

To understand Zen, you must live it.

William Irving

Book: On desire

An unnatural ability to spend moments in moments.

William Irving

Book: On desire

We've forgotten how to just be.

Some, on hearing this description of enlightenment, will ridicule the person who can find pleasure gazing at the smoke drifting up from the tailpipes of the cars blocking his way. Such a person is at best childlike and at worst a fool. They will pity him. But who is more to be pitied, the person who is almost incapable of satisfaction and must therefore spend unsatisfying days in pursuit of a moment or two of satisfaction, or the person who can find satisfaction in the most ordinary moments and whose days are therefore filled with satisfying moments?

William Irving

Book: On desire

The desert, of course, is no less natural than the forest.

James Carse

Book: Finite and infinite games

Genuine travel has no destination. Travelers do not go somewhere, but constantly discover they are somewhere else.

James Carse

Book: Finite and infinite games

What is your body thinking right now?

Genuine travelers travel not to overcome distance but to discover distance.

James Carse

Book: Finite and infinite games

The only time I feel fear as others do is when I think of you in harm.

Lucius Hunt

Movie: The Village

The nature of the sun is to shine.

Rupert Spira

Book: The nature of consciousness

Awareness is the prerequisite for all experience.

Rupert Spira

Book: The nature of consciousness

Awareness is not simply the ultimate reality of experience; it is the only reality of experience.

Rupert Spira

Book: The nature of consciousness

Like a character in a movie that travels the world in search of the screen.

Rupert Spira

Book: The nature of consciousness

Something that has no dimensions is not a thing.

Rupert Spira

Book: The nature of consciousness

In the pause between two thoughts.

Rupert Spira

Book: The nature of consciousness

Somewhere in between quiet and solitude. What I miss most is stillness.

Christopher Knight in Michael Finkel

Book: Stranger in the woods

Mindfulness is the mind's strength, and awareness is its flexibility.

Sakyong Mipham Rinpoche

Book: Running with the Mind of Meditation

Treatments originates from outside, whereas healing comes from within.

Andrew Weil

Book: 8 weeks to optimum health

I wish I may, I wish I might. Wish I was a thousand miles from here tonight.

Caleb

Movie: Near Dark

Are we fitted to the times we're born into?

Lincoln

Movie: Lincoln

The sadness of a single shoe.

Alexandra Horowitz

Book: On looking

Do not let your spirit be influenced by your body, or your body be influenced by your spirit. Be neither insufficiently spirited nor over spirited.

Miyamoto Musashi

Book: The Book of Five Rings

To what makes life most worth living.

Todd Kashdan

Book: Curious?

A wind of invisible voices.

Miss Dolores

TV-Series: True Detective

Religions are only temporary successful attempts to cope with the lack of meaning in life.

Mihaly Csikszentmihaly

Book: Flow

The universe was not designed with the comfort of human beings in mind.

Mihaly Csikszentmihaly

Book: Flow

The always exciting joys of spiritual growth.

Mihaly Csikszentmihaly

Book: The evolving self

Those who seek consolation in existing churches often pay for their peace of mind with a tacit agreement to ignore a great deal of what is known about the way the world works.

Mihaly Csikszentmihaly

Book: Flow

There can be no religion without a church.

Mihaly Csikszentmihaly

Book: The evolving self

God was redundant because the explanation was complete without him.

Julian Baggini

Book: The Philosopher's toolkit

The view from nowhere.

Julian Baggini

Book: The Philosopher's toolkit

There's no point in being unhappy about things you can't change, and no point being unhappy about things you can.

Dan Harris

Book: 10% Happier

One cannot remain equally open to all possibilities or else one ends up believing nothing.

Julian Baggini

Book: What's it all about?

Giving equal credence to every alternative is to have not so much an open mind as an empty one.

Julian Baggini

Book: What's it all about?

Silence is the break in narrative through which deep rhythms and emotions emerge.

What motivates the desire to protect this kind of mystery is, I think, often a kind of fear: a fear that if we cannot depend on there being a God, an afterlife, a soul and values other than those we hold, then we have to take responsibility for making what we can of what is probably the one life we have.

Julian Baggini

Book: What's it all about?

The appeal of 'new age' ideas is based on their promise of something transcendent, since the ideas themselves are largely nonsense.

Julian Baggini

Book: What's it all about?

The first is that such faith is by its nature non-rational. The second is that to have faith does not in any way remove responsibility for one's own ethical and existential decisions.

Julian Baggini

Book: What's it all about?

Love is abstract, but sex is concrete.

But religious believers who risk all on there being an afterlife get no second chance if they are wrong.

Julian Baggini

Book: What's it all about?

An original purpose or lack of purpose does not necessarily fix the purpose of the object for eternity. Purposes can be gained, lost or changed. That is why a consideration of life's origins has not enabled us to come up with any clear answer as to what life's purpose is, and why the naturalist belief that life was not created for a purpose does not mean that life can have no purpose.

Julian Baggini

Book: What's it all about?

Quiet is not merely the absence of noise. Quiet is an affirmative presence. The way sleep is not just the absence of wakefulness, but rather a different state of consciousness, essential to life.

The only remedy for FOMO is to be present.

It is okay to be happy.

Sakyong Mipham Rinpoche

Book: Running with the Mind of Meditation

The choice between good and evil or between right and wrong is no choice at all.

Robert McKee

Book: Story: Substance, Structure, Style, and the Principles of Screenwriting

The first person to say "I love you" has lost because the other, upon hearing it, immediately controls the relationship.

Robert McKee

Book: Story: Substance, Structure, Style, and the Principles of Screenwriting

Not everything pleasurable should be pursued, and not everything that is painful should be avoided.

Because I had a dream last night and In my dream you need the leg and everyone in the world was trying to give you their leg but I really want you to have mine. And in my dream you picked my leg and made me so happy. And it was the best dream in history of dreams.

Sheldon

Movie: I'm Here

Love can be inconvenient, perhaps inappropriate. It can be dangerous. Make us do things we wouldn't dream of doing. But wrong?

Isaak Sirko

TV-Series: Dexter

He was allowed to live in a world of speculation of fantasy, of 'someday' and 'what if'. He never had to gear 'too bad', 'too little or 'too late'.

How not to want what he couldn't have.

Live your life to minimize the regrets you might have at the end.

Gary Keller

Book: The ONE thing

A busy life is not the same as a meaningful one.

Ruth Soukup

Book: Unstuffed

Decide once, and never decide again.

You're afraid that your death may be as meaningless as everyone else's.

Adama

TV-Series: Balllestar Galactica

We confront head on the truth of the thing -the aching preciousness of something we love, of life itself, not despite but because we will lose it.

Being alive we have freedom to exercise our will. And what is will? It's your self-control which is paradoxically the opposite of freedom.

The indifferent stars above.

If I say, "You aren't dead". It's not the same as saying "You are undead". If I say you aren't dead, it simply means you are alive, if I say, "You are undead", it means you are the living dead, you are alive precisely as dead.

Slavoj Zizek

Doc: The reality of the virtual

What kind of a day has it been.

At any given time, you're either moving forward or you're moving backward.

There is no in-between.

Darrin Donnelly

Book: Think like a warrior

We lead different lives for different reasons.

Maester

TV-Series: Game of thrones

The life you live is the life you live regardless if anybody notices or not.

Every day deserves a soundtrack.

My survival is not as important as the survival of things that do not have a limited life expectancy, such as mankind or planet earth. Hence the more "systemic" things are, the more important survival becomes.

Nassim Nicholas Taleb

Book: Skin the game

We are starting to view our world - our reality - like we view a TV program. Like the action is somehow removed from us and is not real. At risk of taking ourselves too seriously.

When you're surrounded by such brilliance, every morning is a reminder to be the very best you can be, and every night is a time to get excited about what's to come.

You're older than you think. Don't learn that the hard way.

Charlie Skinner

TV-Series: The Newsroom

How far in the past do you live?

David Eagleman

Book: Incognito

If you have a limited number of meals left, for example, why would you order a completely new dish you've never tried before, running the risk that you'll hate it, when you can order something you know you like?

Daniel J. Levitin

Book: Organized mind

I had never learned how to enjoy life, only how to achieve. All my life I had been busy seeking happiness, but never finding or sustaining it.

Dan Millman

Book: Peaceful Warrior

Life is not terrible because we live in a hostile world. The tragedy of life is that no one is paying any attention.

The passionate life may itself be the rational way to live.

First of all, we are alive.

Sakyong Mipham Rinpoche

Book: Running with the Mind of Meditation

For better or worse, YOLO

The divine gift does not come from a higher power but from our own minds.

Dr. Ford

TV-Series: Westworld

Living on purpose.

Live in such a way that if someone spoke badly of you, no one would believe it.

The point of being alive is to be there for it.

Sakyong Mipham Rinpoche

Book: Running with the Mind of Meditation

The lives you aren't living.

But this is what we do, who we are. Live for nothing, or die for something.

John J. Rambo

Movie: Rambo

Death is always pointless, that is the point.

Anubis

TV-Series: Gargoyles

I want to watch my life like it's a movie, have to watch it twice.

Each of us actually does have a finite period of time here on this earth; we just don't live like we do.

You don't choose a life. You live one.

Daniel

Movie: The Way

When a storm is over, is it happiness? Or is it just a relief?

Alicia Florrick

TV-Series: The Good Wife

Caleb: What'll we do now?

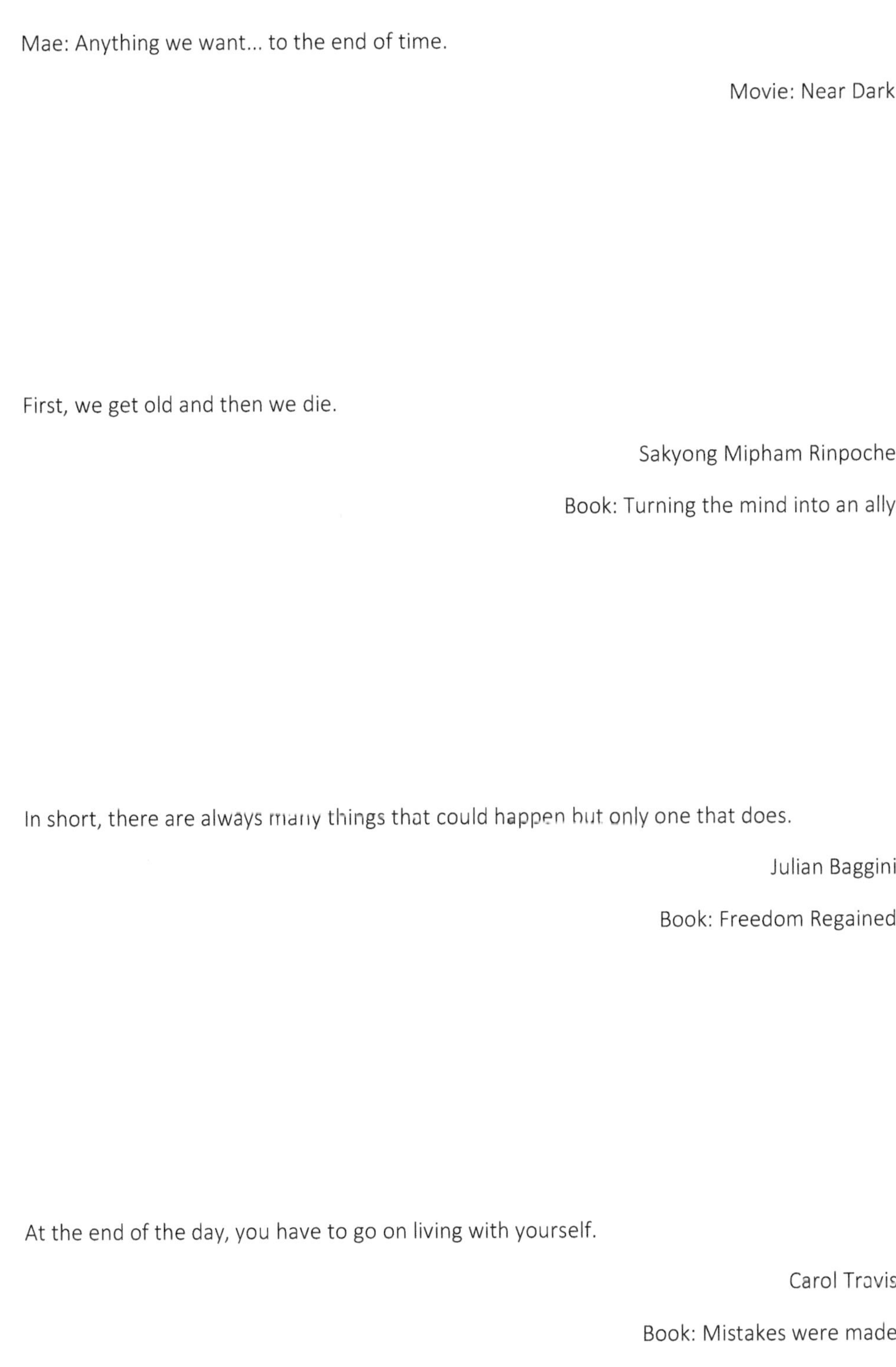

Mae: Anything we want... to the end of time.

Movie: Near Dark

First, we get old and then we die.

Sakyong Mipham Rinpoche

Book: Turning the mind into an ally

In short, there are always many things that could happen but only one that does.

Julian Baggini

Book: Freedom Regained

At the end of the day, you have to go on living with yourself.

Carol Travis

Book: Mistakes were made

The fact of death puts a limit on what we can have, what we can do.

Sakyong Mipham Rinpoche

Book: Turning the mind into an ally

All the possible lives he had rejected.

Kerry Howley

Book: Thrown

The journey is what brings us happiness not the destination.

Dan Millman

Movie: Peaceful Warrior

Clementine: What do we do?

Joel: Enjoy it.

Movie: Eternal Sunshine of the spotless mind

The past is written, impossible to change. Why are so many of us living in the past, living with the shame of what we have done, when we could live in awe of what we might do? What we might do.

Dr. Gaius Baltar

TV-Series: Battlestar Galactica

My sole advantage in life is that I know some of my weaknesses.

Nassim Nicholas Taleb

Book: Fooled by randomness

Live it.

The unlived live.

One of a good-enough life, one where we don't spend our time obsessively analyzing our character or our faults, not over-striving or lamenting what we have not accomplished or become, not constantly feeling that we should have a better life. The notion of settling into, not settling for, the life we have and living it as gratifyingly and graciously as possible.

And if there's no fun to be had, I'm not interested.

Raymond 'Red' Reddington

TV-Series: The Blacklist

An attitude of "if only" keeps a person from living her actual life and instead ties her more to a future possible life that may never be.

Distracted by the mundane interruptions of daily life, we forget our main purpose. It's simply to live.

Tools to prove you are alive, but not to make you feel more alive.

Simply by being here.

Everything lead me to this point.

Living beyond the expected.

Death does a better job than anyone or anything at teaching us how to live.

Life is serialized. Life is not a procedural.

Damon Lindelof

Doc: Showrunners

Nothing distinguishes memories from ordinary moments. Only later do they become memorable by the scar they leave.

If you have a problem with your ending, the answer always lies in the beginning.

Syd Field

Book: Screenplay

A permanent solution to a temporary problem.

Life is about progress, not perfection.

All our biological bodies are limited and we need to deal with overcoming limitations, one means or another. There is nothing good about disease and death as much as we try to ennoble it.

Ray Kurzweil

Documentary: The transcendent man

Lives are for the Living.

Narrator

Book: Machine of Death

My life extends far beyond the limitations of me.

Robert Frobisher

Movie: Cloud Atlas

Living life to the fullest.

Sustainable pleasure.

What surprised me was the freedom which habits gave me.

Tynan

Book: Superhuman by habit

While not exceptional, our life is not identical to anybody else. It is our life -nobody else's.

Joshua Becker

Book: Simplify

We are unlikely to have a good and meaningful life unless we can overcome our insatiability.

William Braxton Irving

Book: A guide to the good life

We should periodically interrupt our enjoyment of what life has to offer to spend time contemplating the loss of whatever it is we are enjoying.

William Braxton Irving

Book: A guide to the good life

Whenever we desire something that is not up to us, our tranquility will likely be disrupted.

William Braxton Irving

Book: A guide to the good life

Most of us have two lives. The life we live and the unlived life within us.

Steven Pressfield

Book: The war of art

Pause to consider its cosmic (in)significance.

William Braxton Irving

Book: A guide to the good life

The question isn't, whether self-disciplined and duty-bound people can have a happy, meaningful life; it is whether those who lack self-control and who are convinced that nothing is bigger than they can have such a life.

William Braxton Irving

Book: A guide to the good life

You simply "live" and not "live for."

Bruce Lee

Book: Striking thoughts

To live now you must die to yesterday.

Bruce Lee

Book: Striking thoughts

We exist in order to be happy (and meaningful).

You just had to be there.

Bill Bowerman

Doc: Prefontaine

The things you're most afraid of have already happened.

Sy Parrish

Movie: One Hour Photo

Life, unfortunately, isn't always lived under the best conditions.

David McRaney

Book: You are not so smart

Life is better lived than conceptualized.

Bruce Lee

Book: Striking thoughts

For the ride of a lifetime.

Phil Knight

Book: Shoe dog

Because I honestly wished I could do it all over again.

Phil Knight

Book: Shoe dog

In our efforts to not miss anything, we unwittingly miss everything.

Brian P. Moran

Book: The 12 Week year

Have some fun along the way.

There is only ever going to be one you. Ever. You are absolutely perfect at being you.

Both the regret and the honest wish I could do it all over again... and yet I know I can't.

And yet I know that this regret clashes with my secret regret -that I can't do it all over again.

Phil Knight

Book: Shoe dog

Too young to be old.

So much to do. So much to learn. So much I don't know about my own life.

Phil Knight

Book: Shoe dog

When one says that thought exists, it automatically includes saying that one exists because there is no thought that does not contain as one of its elements a subject who thinks.

Bruce Lee

Book: Striking thoughts

We do not live in the past, but the past in us.

Thomas Sowell

Book: Economic fallacies and facts

Unlike a clock and other human designs, a complex system is never finished, never has a "final" shape.

Nicholas Nassim Taleb

l ive focused.

Everyday parties.

The person who sacrifices too much enjoyment of life to serve the purpose of future wealth and security is thus making the mistake of overestimating the extent to which his future life will be better than the one he could have now.

Julian Baggini

Book: What's it all about?

Dying could be understood to be the paradoxical goal of life.

Natasha Dow Schüll

Book: Addicted by design

The life of pleasure thus become a kind of toil, because you are either enjoying yourself or you are nothing.

Julian Baggini

Book: What's it all about?

A distraction free life.

If it is the seeking that counts, it undermines the importance of the very thing that we are supposed to be searching for.

Julian Baggini

Book: What's it all about?

If you are not enjoying the journey, you probably won't enjoy the destination.

Chris Lear

Book: Running with the buffaloes

Living life forwards.

Julian Baggini

Book: What's it all about?

Live like no one else.

Dave Ramsey

Book: The total money makeover

When your spider-sense can no longer protect you? When your clock starts to tick, what happens then? The mundane becomes spectacular.

Peter Parker

Comic: The Amazing Spiderman The Other

Let's make some rare moments, together.

Sam Lustgarten

Book: Frugaling

Decadence means that you no longer have an appetite for great adventures, but it does not mean that you no longer want to survive.

George Friedman

Book: The next 100 years

For a living. For fun. To make life interesting.

Xela

Book: 14

I want to be happy for the "right reasons."

Living one day at a time.

Mr. Brooks

Movie: Mr. Brooks

And if I don't want to die, I've got to start living.

Anna Fox

Book: The woman in the window

Your life is a reflection of the stories you tell. Be a good storyteller.

Jerry Lynch

Book: The way of the champion

Zero regrets.

Jerry Lynch

Book: The way of the champion

A life well lived.

Danny Dover

Book: The minimalist mindset

The eccentric is implying that he is somehow outside -or even worse, above-the "rules" of the society in which he lives. The rest of us have to conform to societal expectations.

William Irving

Book: On desire

The meaning of life is life itself.

If you are willing to accept "Crazy" as part of your nickname, you can live the life of your own choosing rather than having to conform to the expectations of those around you.

William Irving

Book: On desire

Infinite players cannot say when their game began, nor do they care. They do not care for the reason that their game is not bounded by time. Indeed, the only purpose of the game is to prevent it coming to an end, to keep everyone in play.

James Carse

Book: Finite and infinite games

They enter into finite games with all the appropriate energy and self-veiling, but they do so without the seriousness of finite players. They embrace the abstractness of finite games as abstractness, and therefore take them up not seriously, but playfully.

James Carse

Book: Finite and infinite games

If we all live forever we never have to make a choice on anything.

My daily routine: get up, be amazing, go back to bed.

We all die eventually. The real tragedy is forgetting to live.

Dr. Melinda Bird

TV-Series: Legion

One day is all days.

Ryan Holiday

Book: The daily stoic

Living without restriction.

Ryan Holiday

Book: The daily stoic

Life isn't about searching endlessly to find what's missing; it's about learning to live with the missing parts.

Michael Finkel

Book: Stranger in the woods

Everyone leaves a trace.

Michael Finkel

Book: Stranger in the woods

He lived for a living.

Michael Finkel

Book: Stranger in the woods

For some people, the pain inflicted by self-harm is preferable to the numbness and emptiness that it replaces -it is something rather than nothing, and a salutatory reminder that one is still able to feel, that one is still alive. For others, the pain of self-harm merely replaces a different kind of pain that they can neither understand nor control.

To improve life one must improve the quality of experience.

Mihaly Csikszentmihaly

Book: Flow

Attention is our most important tool in the task of improving the quality of experience.

Mihaly Csikszentmihaly

Book: Flow

To free inner life from the threat of chaos.

Mihaly Csikszentmihaly

Book: Flow

The fear of death is the result of being too closely identified with an individual self.

Mihaly Csikszentmihaly

Book: The evolving self

Life becomes serene and enjoyable precisely when selfish pleasure and personal success are no longer the guiding goals.

Mihaly Csikszentmihaly

Book: The evolving self

To live an entire life without understanding how we think, why we feel the way we feel, what directs our actions is to miss what is most important in life, which is the quality of experience itself.

Mihaly Csikszentmihaly

Book: The evolving self

Everyday life in utopia.

Gretchen Rubin

Book: Better than before

Maybe we're distracting ourselves from the fact that we're dying.

When you realize how quickly everything can fall apart, it makes you never want to give up anything good ever again.

Wallace

Movie: What if

Life can and does have meaning. It doesn't have meaning in itself, from a neutral perspective. But it means something to us.

Julian Baggini

Book: What's it all about?

The only thing to do with life is to enjoy it.

Joyce Meyer

Book: Making Good Habits, Breaking Bad Habits

The most intense aesthetic experiences actually have their power precisely because they remind us of our mortality.

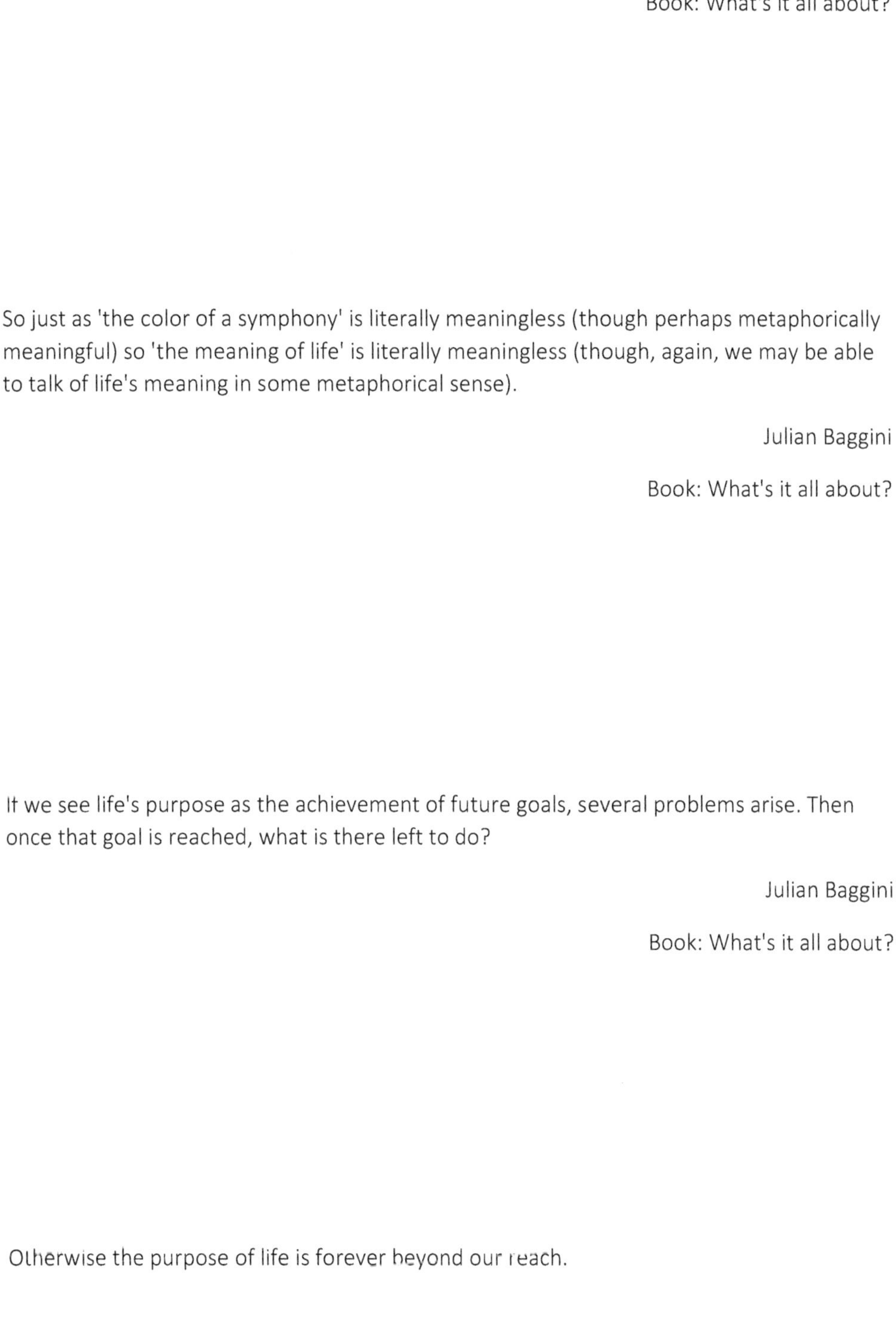

Julian Baggini

Book: What's it all about?

So just as 'the color of a symphony' is literally meaningless (though perhaps metaphorically meaningful) so 'the meaning of life' is literally meaningless (though, again, we may be able to talk of life's meaning in some metaphorical sense).

Julian Baggini

Book: What's it all about?

It we see life's purpose as the achievement of future goals, several problems arise. Then once that goal is reached, what is there left to do?

Julian Baggini

Book: What's it all about?

Otherwise the purpose of life is forever beyond our reach.

Julian Baggini

Book: What's it all about?

Lifspeki. The philosophy by which one lives their life. In essence, you can have a philosophy you believe in, but don't act upon. The philosophy you produce through those actions, is your lifspeki.

Celebrating life.

Sakyong Mipham Rinpoche

Book: Running with the Mind of Meditation

All men must die, but first we'll live.

Ygrette

Book: Game of Thrones

The path you've set for me is full of hurdles where the answer comes before the question.

Jean Claude Van Damme

Movie: JCVD

Let's make sure that we enjoy these moments and try to share as many as we can together.

The crossroad of decision, the place where we have the chance to incorporate what we learned from our guides.

About the author

Víctor de la Fuente, born in Barcelona in 1982, has an extensive professional career in the digital field while sport and travel have marked his philosophy of life.

On the professional side, the author has combined his core professional career with entrepreneurship and training. In his main job he has had the opportunity to work for companies of different sizes and nature such as Nestlé, Adevinta or Groupalia and Veepee to mention a few. To his main activity, he adds consulting services through his own agency vdelafuente where he collaborates with companies also from different sectors and with very different needs always in the field of digital marketing and eCommerce. In addition, Víctor de la Fuente actively collaborates with different universities such as the University of Barcelona, as well as different business schools such as MIOTI or ISDI, among others, as a professor in different masters and postgraduate courses. In his professional career, he also has experience as an entrepreneur co-founding, among others, a fashion application in startup mode along with two other founders.

On the personal side, Victor de la Fuente's life is marked mainly by a trip around the world where he carried only a backpack for 7 months. His life is also marked by his dedication to sports, especially running, where he has participated in numerous marathons and mountain ultramarathons. All this has given him a unique vision of life mixing stoicism, Buddhism and essentialism, among other philosophies.

Other books by the author

Published in English:

- 365 quotes and meditations. English version. Víctor de la Fuente. 2021
- Against utopía. English version. Víctor de la Fuente. 2022
- Digital detox. English version. Víctor de la Fuente. 2020
- Minimalism: live better with less (and achieve mental quietness). English version. Víctor de la Fuente. 2016
- Poems from a metal heart. English version. Víctor de la Fuente. 2021
- Smart Simple Investment Strategy. English version. Víctor de la Fuente. 2021
- Stoicism and Zen Buddhism in Modern Life. English version. Víctor de la Fuente. 2023

Publicados en castellano:

- Aprende a Invertir. Versión en castellano. Víctor de la Fuente. 2021
- Ciberacoso: un problema IRL. Versión en castellano. Víctor de la Fuente. 2023
- Contra la utopía. Versión en castellano. Víctor de la Fuente. 2022
- Detox digital. Versión en castellano. Víctor de la Fuente. 2020
- Estoicismo y budismo zen en la vida moderna. Versión en castellano. Víctor de la Fuente. 2023
- La estrategia win y otros ensayos de la economía digital. Versión en castellano. Víctor de la Fuente. 2023
- Minimalismo: vivir mejor con menos y lograr calma mental. Versión en castellano. Víctor de la Fuente. 2016